Elegy for Emily

By the same author:

Elegy for Emily

A Verse Biography of
Emily Remler (1957–1990)

Geoff Page

PUNCHER & WATTMANN

First published in 2019

Published by Puncher and Wattmann

PO Box 279

Waratah NSW 2298

http://www.puncherandwattmann.com

puncherandwattmann@bigpond.com

 A catalogue record for this book is available from the National Library of Australia

ISBN   9781925780253

Cover design by Miranda Douglas

Cover photo: Brian McMillen

Printed by Lightning Source International

This project has been assisted by the Australian Government through the Australia Council, its arts funding and advisory body.

Australian Government

1.

As for getting into music, I've been doing that since I was three
when my father says I wrote three songs on the piano and, the
way he puts it, two of them were great.

Born or made? we always ask.
It's not too hard to see her there,
prodigious little three-year-old,

back in 1960,
Manhattan-born, New Jersey-bred,
parents Jewish, well set-up,

Emily, the third of three.
Older brother plays guitar,
a Gibson ES-330.

He's not as keen as little Em
and finds that she's detached it from him.
Two decades on it still will be

the one she uses most.
Already though she's on acoustic
and playing folk at nine.

Her drawing and her painting
aren't much less important.
Her mother though, described as 'housewife',

likes to say, 'Achieve. Do well.'
Elsewhere, Mom's described as having
worked in 'social services'.

And later Emily will think
her mother maybe made
a bit 'too much of that',

the need for doggedness, that is.
At first it's folk; then rock.
Em doesn't practise much although

she has a nimble ear and soon
is playing Hendrix songs
picked out on one string only.

For grade school it's the local:
'Jewish and Italian kids'.
For high school she is bussed

to Englewood to mix the shades.
The black kids aren't too friendly though.
'They beat us up' and 'stole our money'

even though she's 'into blues'.
She calls herself a little 'hippie'
and takes to cutting classes

and so is sent to Windsor Mountain,
a boarding school in Massachussetts,
'alternative', 'experimental'.

And in what proves to be its
next-to-final year.
It's here, at fifteen years of age,

that Emily begins to plan
a lifetime playing blues.
She's listening to B.B. King,

Johnny Winter, 'all those people'.
She does a music camp as well.
Her ear is 'weird'; she finds she has

no trouble singing note-for-note
the Ravi Shankar records
they put in front of her.

At sixteen now, it's either
graphic arts (Rhode Island) or
music (Berklee College,

Boston, Massachussetts).
The latter's where she gets the nod.
'It's easy to get into Berklee,'

she says. 'But staying in is hard.'

2.

*I partied a lot at Berklee. There were 50 men to every woman. You
bring out a cigarette and you get 10 lights.*

She takes two years when most take four.
At eighteen she's a graduate,
despite the 'partying'.

Shy about her chops at first,
it takes her months to front her teacher.
She gets her theory nailed though,

'the what you need to learn and then
forget,' she's fond of saying later,
quoting Miles, not quite verbatim.

And as for those ten guys with lighters,
there's not much on the record.
Towards the end we know at least

she has a boyfriend, Steve,
who's up there from New Orleans;
a 'monster' on guitar, she says.

Who, as they leave, persuades her into
moving south with him,
to live and gig amid the music's

humid origins.
'It took me time to get to like it,'
she's happy to confess re jazz.

Miles and Coltrane 33s
seem like noise at first.
'It was just a bunch of notes to me.'

A friend, Chuck Loeb, teaches her
how and what to listen for.
Charlie Christian is a start,

the guy who starred with Benny Goodman,
and died at twenty-six.
She tracks Paul Desmond down on alto,

that laid-back, 'dry martini'
clarity of line.
And Wes Montgomery, of course,

after whom the path was clear.
She puts his poster on the wall,
this man who'd died in '68,

a guy she'd never met,
a man she 'knew' though through his music.
She starts by learning fragments:

two bars, four bars, hard transcriptions,
the fingering by listening for
the timbre of each string.

She steals, without apology,
his unique way with octaves,
his low-down warm and bluesy sound,

the sparks of humour too.
'I may look like a nice Jewish girl'
she often jokes with interviewers,

'but inside there's a heavy-set
black man waiting to get out.'
It's almost like a mantra.

In '89 she's saying still:
'I'm not so sure I ever got
as good as Wes.' She knows

the weight of what she's chosen.

3.

I stopped in Long Beach Island on the shore in New Jersey, and
rented a room, and proceeded to quit smoking, and learn to play.

All that summer, just eighteen,
eight weeks straight, eight hours a day,
one room on that New Jersey shore

and one electric fan,
the cigarettes put by as well.
She sheds eleven kilos and

recalls she 'swam a lot'.
Her boyfriend, Steve, is in New Orleans
but she's not ready yet.

'Willpower's not the question,'
she tells us more than once.
It's here she gets it all together,

the harmony she's learnt at Berklee,
the two-bar, four-bar, eight-bar phrases
lifted off the vinyl.

It's not known how the neighbours felt;
eight hours straight of chords and runs
coming through a wall or window

intercut with John Coltrane
while others tan beside the surf
and check the passing talent.

A summer school for one;
an autodidact, it would seem,
but with a fiery teacher.

Perhaps she plays her latest licks
long-distance down the phone
although her money, we surmise,

wouldn't run to that.
Self-discipline, hard work.
It's maybe in the genes, Em thinks.

'I had a lot of ideas but
I still wasn't very good'.
Perfectionists, it's true,

are prone to modesty.

4.

It wasn't till I got to New Orleans that I started getting good.

Three years down south she lives with Steve;
hears him practise through the wall
and sees she's catching up.

She takes the gigs that he can't do
and all the others she can manage.
She's not a purist though;

bebop's just one choice from many.
'If I had stayed in Boston,'
she says in '82,

'I'd be playing "Giant Steps" like
a madman — like everybody else.'
No, she's happy at The Fairmont,

relaxing in its plush,
backing all the Vegas acts,
Robert Gourlay, Nancy Wilson,

and brushing up her reading.
She's in a band where she's the only
girl. Or person under sixty.

New Orleans trad, all black and classic,
unchanged for eighty years.
And all the while she has her students,

25 of them a week.
She's in a band with Steve called 'Fourplay'.
She digs New Orleans R&B;

also the local soul
and gigs with Little Queenie &
the Percolators, loud and sweaty.

There's nothing in all this that doesn't
bring her something new,
more blessings from the Crescent City.

Her band's hired for an oyster bar;
the management's not too concerned
exactly what they play.

The pay is partly 'shrimps and oysters',
They jam each night as 'long and late'
as Em might have a mind to.

Her love for Steve runs three years only.
In '82 she's quoted saying:
'my boyfriend in New Orleans

isn't any more.'
And offers us the words:
'As soon as I was getting good

we had to scratch each other.'

5.

Anyway he said to come up and I did and we played all afternoon.

A spot of luck. And chutzpah too.
Herb Ellis is in town
and playing at le Club.

One of her guitars, the one
that wears his famous name,
has had a problem lately.

She rings him up from nowhere much
and asks if he can help,
Herb Ellis who had held the spot

with Oscar Peterson for years,
a man with equals maybe
but no superiors.

She asks him for a lesson too.
And so they 'play all afternoon'.
It's just the break a girl could wish for.

And hard work deserve.
'I'll make you a star,' we're told he said.
Three weeks later she's on stage

at Concord, California,
up there with 'The Great Guitars':
Herb Ellis, Barney Kessel,

Tal Farlow, Charlie Byrd.
'And little me,' she adds,
a smile still shining in the words

thirty-five years later.
Within a year she's 'sideman' on
a record cut for Concord.

Carl Jefferson, the owner,
signs her up for what will prove
a neat half-dozen of her own

across the next eight years.
'I'm not a finished package yet,'
she notes in half-apology.

'I'm still a little kid.'

6.

Perhaps I'm a true Virgo. I like things very neat.

It's back to the Big Apple now;
she's taken what she's needed from
Louisiana's 'Crescent City'.

Soon she's backing Nancy Wilson
playing at Carnegie Hall.
Astrud Gilberto wants her too.

Em's got the samba and the bossa
nailed although she's not seen Rio.
She knows just where the accents fall

and how to please a singer —
just a 'presence', not too much.
She holds the gig three years.

The YouTube clips today
preserve her there at work,
smiling quietly into space

beside the well-dressed Astrud.
For Emily, accompaniment
has never been a step-down.

Keep your profile 'low', she says,
'make someone else sound good.'
She's 'so in love with it'

she almost turns Brazilian
by musical osmosis.
Carlos Jobim, Joao Gilberto ...

she's got the style beneath her fingers.
'Triste', 'How Insensitive',
'The Girl from Ipanema'.

For her it's not an either/or,
bebop or the bossa.
Her trio's at the Blue Note too.

She's sitting-in round town.
In '81 she's flying west;
another piece of luck.

One guy from her twenty students
learns the Emily arrangement
of Duke's tune, 'Satin Doll';

turns out his father is producing
Sophisticated Ladies. Em
is hired to join the orchestra

and make the long jump to L.A.
where the show will run a season.
By '86 she's vague on detail.

''82 or '83,'
she's telling Martin Richards,
boasting just a little of her

playing with those 'names',
the men who'd toured with Duke himself,
Lawrence Brown and Snooky Young,

Marshall Royal. Plus Herman Riley,
'another great tenor player ...
that people might not know.'

'30-odd musicians',
not to mention dancers,
out there on the 'coast'

remembering the Cotton Club
of Harlem in the thirties.
She has no bother with the charts;

She's always been a 'reader'.
Sophisticated Ladies
is Broadway, pure and absolute,

lines of black, long-legged dancers,
tunes to whistle later
walking to the car;

the Ellington & Strayhorn Songbook
restored to centre-stage,
and Emily along there with them

adding to the bite and texture.
Back home, before and after,
she's studying Coltrane

who's died when she was nine.
She knows there's still a way to go.
She's working on the pianists too —

Tyner and Bill Evans.
She gets a second gig at Concord,
another in Berlin.

In 1981 she joins
the band of Monty Alexander,
a pianist from Jamaica

who's earned his place already
and played with all the names.
He too is 'neat' like Emily

and digs in deep to swing.
It really ought not matter but
he's thirteen years her senior,

born on D-Day, '44.

7.

It was hard to be married and on the road. We had haphazard
meetings. We had to get used to each other again.

Each marriage is a sort of secret;
Emily's and Monty's
just a little more so.

Convergences, divergences ...
and mutual respect
which long outlives the split.

In one of Leonard Feather's
famous blindfold tests
she guesses Monty right first time;

gets Barney Kessel too.
'Monty was burning, wasn't he?'
We see the almost girlish smile.

'Be sure you put that in.
I'm very relieved I got that one.
On a social level,' she adds.

She's right there in his band at first,
antiphonal to his piano,
but neither is a shadow.

Opportunities arrive,
forestall their prior agreements.
They plan to rendezvous in Paris.

Occasionally, it happens.
In '82, still married,
she's telling People magazine

that, now she's made her first LP,
her parents take her seriously:
'At least they've given up on me

getting married and having children.'
It hardly matters who
began divorce proceedings.

A journalist, some four years later,
reports: 'They are just friends,
albeit good ones.' It can't have been

so very easy. In '88
she tells Gene Lees about it,
leisurely, in some detail.

'After the divorce,' she says,
'I played great for a while
on all that pain. I really did.

I also tried to destroy myself
as fast as I could'. And how was that?
we're asking — unentitled.

She's telling Lees how some great talents
'often have a dark side'.
'It's very easy to see,' she smiles,

'the good side when you're doing bad.'
When and where exactly is it
she starts in 'doing bad'?

When and why that first syringe?

8.

But when I'm playing I forget whether I'm a girl or a boy or a cat.

By 1984 or so
her novelty is almost gone.
Girl a singer? Say no more.

Women on the jazz piano
go back to 1925 —
Lil Hardin on the Armstrong sides.

But modern jazz guitar? Whoa there!
The journalists can't pass it up.
Has it been a boon or burden?

Some detect 'a turmoil ...
behind her calm expression';
assure her that she has a touch

'uniquely feminine'.
Jazz, they know, is more than hard
and 'doubly tough' for women.

Yet always Em comes batting back,
never less than honest.
'Being a woman has worked both for

and against me,' she concedes.
For you if you're 'pretty good',
against you if you're not.'

Though not a 'looker' Em has charm
that draws male journalists like moths.
Some become protective,

avuncular at times.
Intensity like hers, for them,
will always be a worry.

The issue never fades away.
'I have to prove myself
every single time,'

she notes in '85.
She's always known technique alone
can never be enough.

'I'll go up there,' she likes to boast,
'and burn their asses off.'
'And are you doing it for women?'

some gents feel bound to ask.
'You don't get feminist,' she says.
'You just get so damned good

that they'll forget about that crap.'
Initially, her clothes at work
don't differ much from men's.

She's not a singer, after all;
no need to show the shoulders.
Later, grown more confident,

she'll 'wear a dress on stage.'
And sometimes shed her shoes.
The journalists still fall about

and note: 'The dark-haired Miss Remler
sits on the edge of a stool'.
'Emily was wearing

black slacks and a white blouse.'
She doesn't close them out however.
She knows that what they write means money.

'I love dresses but I love
baggy pants too. It's strictly a matter
of comfort.' It's clear she's been compelled

to think about the issue.
Was Wes Montgomery ever asked,
she must have thought from time to time,

dumb questions such as these?
'Music is sexless,' she declares.
'I think everyone

has something that is feminine
and something that is masculine.'
She's always known the expectations.

Her weight has varied with the years.
'I was raised to think if I was thin
people would like me more.'

In time, she finds she now accepts
her 'body has a tendency
to be a certain weight.'

She can get worried though for others
and sometimes likes to preach.
'A lot of women in this world

are using drugs to stay thin ...
they're killing themselves to be
fifteen pounds lighter and please

American society.'
The interviews are often lazy,
drifting here and there,

retelling worn-out stories.
Sometimes though they scrape
on something hard — a sudden reef

that neither has intended.

9.

As you might imagine, I've had a lot of requests to play with
all-female groups. And when I was twenty-one, some very good
musicians had this band and asked me to do a gig in Michigan,
good money and just one set.'

She's twenty-one and money talks.
It's not a trend Em has much time for,
the all-girl band. She knows however

there are women playing now
not unlike herself,
women with the chops to cut it

up on-stage with men. The lakes
of Michigan in summer prove
a chance to leave New York behind.

'It was eight thousand gay women'.
She doesn't list the instruments
or name the other players

except to call them 'good musicians'.
Em has, we know, backed major females:
Nancy Wilson, Astrud and

the sweeter Rosemary Clooney.
The Michigan experience ...
proves 'enlightening',

a view of beauty stranger than
the one Hugh Hefner spins,
women who'd 'desexed the language'.

'Womon/Womyn'. Not just spelling.
'I felt weird' she does admit.
'Although there were some things I really

loved about it.' 'No bullshitting'
for a start. She segues to
a sort of rant re women who

'stick fingers down their throat,'
the schoolgirls who have 'complexes
about being thin.' 'I had that problem,'

she confesses to Gene Lees
much later *sans* embarrassment.
The worries of a schoolgirl linger

fifteen years and more.
A fluency on jazz guitar,
the love-shout of an audience,

will never quite subdue them.

10.

I heard Mary Osborne once and she sounded great.

Emily Remler / Mary Osborne,
more than thirty years apart,
Mary Osborne who had jammed

with Charlie Christian once.
Who smiled and told her not to 'rush'.
She'd come up through the thirties,

an early convert to the amp,
essentially a swing musician
with bebop added later

on 52nd Street
playing with the men who'd heard
a world shift underneath them.

Married to a trumpeter,
she had three children in four years
across her later thirties,

her first full-length LP recorded
pregnant with the third.
Musicians whom she played with form

a powerful resumé:
Ben Webster, Coleman Hawkins,
Big Joe Turner, Dizzy Gillespie,

Marian McPartland,
Jo Jones and Tommy Flanagan.
She jammed with Lionel Hampton too

and not long after died of cancer.
In later years, she'd run a business
with her husband, Ralph Scaffidi,

guitars and amplifiers,
in Bakersfield, CA.
It's said she used to say to him:

'The house needs cleaning but
I have to practice now'.
'I never got a job,' she claimed,

'because I was a girl'.
Gene Lees, who bailed her up
towards the end, declared

Mary was the only woman
he'd ever heard in jazz
to not complain of bias.

She and Emily comprise
a neatly savage contrast,
Emily's whole life contained

within the last three decades of
Mary's more relaxed one.
It's telling too that Emily

didn't speak of Mary much
in all those interviews
though both of them acknowledged

a black man who'd died young.

11.

For my two musical personalities: the modern me, and the bebop me.

For all those men in music shops,
the aspirant guitarists,
and women too at times,

equipment is the key.
A Gibson ES-330
belonging to her brother

is where Em starts at nine
and plays it ever after.
She likes the size of it;

it's not 'too fat' to get around.
In 1984 or so
she adds a Borys B120,

hollow body. Her strings are all
D'Addario elevens,
used with extra-heavy picks.

Her amps are Musicman
or Polytone, although she will
use others (Fender, Roland)

should they be on-stage already.
They're always light enough to carry
'otherwise I get strange men ...

to help me take it out of the car.'

12.

*Miss Remler and her trio will play at the Blue Note (475-8592)
tonight through Sunday at 10 P.M., midnight and 2 A.M. There is a
$6 cover charge and two-drink minimum at tables; $3 cover and one
drink minimum at the bar.*

It's somewhere in the middle eighties.
Emily is at the Blue Note,
perched there on a stool,

drummer to the left
and bassist on the right.
There'll be no music stand in sight.

They'll play, say, fifteen tunes
across a three-set night.
There'll be a bit of murmur

back there at the bar.
The rest are silent at their tables,
slowly nursing drinks

and watching (mainly) Emily,
her eyes shut centre-stage,
the burnish of her Gibson

projecting unpredictably
the downlights on the walls.
Her sidemen are attentive

but half-invisible as well,
watching her for cues.
Em is where the focus is.

At times it's thumb and fingers,
the way Wes used to play,
a plectrum stuck between her lips,

a sight some men complain about —
pretty New York Jewish lass
with plastic in her mouth.

She's confident, but far from brash.
She knows she has the skill required.
Her count-ins are unwavering;

the guys are more than ready.
This set, like the other two,
will be professionally varied:

ballad for a change of tempo,
a new original or two
ready for the next recording,

one blues at least and, yes,
that running but not 'racing'
classic bit of bebop.

She feels the audience come with her.
She wants to 'take them somewhere'
as she herself, in turn,

is looking to be 'taken somewhere'
when listening to others.
Her introductions these days

are neither pert nor shy.
Sometimes they're back-announcements,
confirming tunes the listeners

can't quite put a name on.
Most, but never all,
are experts in the jazz tradition;

they smile and recognise
the riffs pioneered by others.
They know the role that homage plays.

A few stare idly at their drinks
and think about what happens next,
the subway and the small apartment,

the first-date doorway kiss
that may or may not lead upstairs.
Em cares about her listeners

and sets a task that's not too hard,
a recent Broadway hit perhaps,
something they'll be humming later.

Longterm aficionados know
that none of what they hear is easy.
They know that this has been a set

when something unexpected,
and suddenly transcendent, happened.
Once perhaps, three times at most.

They know that this is why they've come
and paid $6 at the door
to watch a beer go flat or ice

dilute a gin and tonic.

13.

Remler Plays In Trance. 'I'm Really Into It,' Says Top Woman Guitarist

Later, in a puff piece,
summer '89,
she's living now at Sheepshead Bay,

out the ocean end of Brooklyn.
'A big safe place on the water,' she's
lovingly described it elsewhere

(Jazztimes, December,'88).
'I can go to the beach.' Then adds,
a little disconcertingly,

'And look for medical supplies.'
She has a sweet-talk way, they say,
with doctors who love jazz.

Today, Nels Nelson, Daily News,
has called her on the phone.
His piece will note the great marina,

the 'Jewish-Italian' neighbourhood.
Emily lives here, Nels reveals,
with 'two guitars, two cats, a boyfriend'.

To Nels she cannot seem but be
a 'breezy Bohemian'.
He runs the standard anecdotes,

seeking confirmation:
the Berklee years, those two months on
the Jersey shore, eight hours a day

developing her chops
and then the three years in New Orleans,
the anecdote about Herb Ellis,

the 'woman thing' (a plus or minus?).
The gig's in Philadelphia,
just a trio, Mike and Rick.

She gets, towards the end, to say
a word on Pat Martino who
is 'Philadelphia-based'.

He might be in the audience.
'A whole new style of jazz guitar,'
she adds and praises how he plays

those 'straight 8th notes' so well.

14.

I was an artist. I did sculpting and drawings.

Eighteen months she lives in Pittsburg.
Her share apartment in Manhattan
has, it seems, gone 'co-op'.

In '88 and '89
she's Resident at Duquesne Uni,
teaching, learning, taking classes.

Composition (Aydin Esen,
David Stock and Bob Brookmeyer).
And just a whiff of electronics.

'I plug the guitar into the amp,'
she says, 'and it's a big deal.'
She'd like to work in film as well

but that's a world that's hard to crack.
She's got the harmony from Berklee
and all that she's done since.

Each album now from Concord has
more Remler compositions.
She likes to talk about her 'fragments'

evolving into songs.
In '85 already she
is talking of John Williams,

Hollywood composer,
and how he can make 'millions'
feel a 'certain way',

to move them as he wishes.
Likewise, Leonard Bernstein,
her 'hero most admired'.

'More than Wes' and 'more than Coltrane'.
'I wouldn't be playing music if
it weren't for *West Side Story*'.

For now though it's a trio,
quartet at the most,
or touring as a solo act

and gigging with the locals who
are often, she'll concede,
quite close to New York levels.

The big screen stays an aspiration.
The way to there's not clear from here
although she knows L.A. a little.

Pittsburg is a 'pretty city',
she'll happily tell people later.
She isn't short of friends.

She misses New York badly though;
that density of top musicians
within a block or two,

the way one just pops into MoMA.

15.

*Our styles were so different but somehow we came together. It was
a nice record and a nice experience and I'll probably be doing
another one in a little while.*

Summer of 1985 —
Emily and Larry
(Coryell, that is)

are touring Europe as a duo
around the time their disc, *Together,*
adds a notch to her career.

A German jazz photographer
has put their photo on the net,
sitting nestled on a sofa,

Emily, half-quizzical,
Larry with large glasses and
a rather goofy smile.

They're looking happy, half-domestic.
And on the wall behind them there's
some rough graffiti saying,

apropos of nothing,
'DRINKINK DRUGS WILL KILL YOU'.
Elsewhere, *Together*'s cover art

shows Emily on Larry's shoulder
smiling at the lens.
Around that time the two of them

are surfacing from breakups.
Wikipedia asserts
(provisionally, of course)

they were 'romantically involved'
and adds the adverb 'briefly',
a phrase also in Larry's memoir

which notes that they 'had little in common'.
Their bodies may have been *Together*
'briefly'. Certainly their minds were,

the microphones set close
for seamless integration,
an early digital recording.

Years later, Coryell recalls,
'She was a natural.' And claims,
'Probably the best guitarist

to come along in her lifetime'.
Which means the 1980s really.
We don't know how the split occurs.

Coryell himself has 'problems'
round about that time.
Chemicals can bring convergence

and then divergence later.
Emily in '86
remembers their relationship

as 'musical'; adds nothing more.
She's proud of their *Transitions*
and talks about the album's 'smoothness'

even though their styles are 'different' —
he from jazz-rock fusion,
she from bebop but they share

the same small group of mentors.
Later, within months,
Em's 'Guitarist of the Year"

in Downbeat magazine.
The anecdote which charms the most
is how that same photographer,

young and feminist in Hamburg,
yells out once between the tunes
the title of Em's LP *Firefly*

back there in the States.
'Remler turns to Coryell,
beaming like a schoolgirl.'

And says, 'She knows my song.'
Thirteen years there were between them,
Emily and Larry,

but never condescension.

16.

All these legendary guys onstage — Herb Ellis, Barney Kessel,
Tal Farlow, Charlie Byrd — and little me.

For most, but not quite all, musicians
(Harry Carney, say)
the list of whom they've played with makes

a lifetime roll of honour or
a CV at the least.
Emily's, through fourteen years,

remains impressive even now.
And this is not to count
those 'local-hero stay-at-homes'

who 'weren't the worst experience',
as Emily, the troubador,
was happy to admit.

Make a list, almost at random.
Strange the way they scan.
Hank Jones, Eddie Gomez,

Marvin 'Smitty' Smith,
Buster Williams, Nancy Wilson,
Monty Alexander,

Barney Kessel, Charlie Byrd
and Larry Coryell,
Sonny Rollins, Freddie Hubbard,

Bob Moses, Cedar Walton,
Pat Martino, Stanley Jordan,
Joe Pass, Rosemary Clooney,

Marsalis brothers (Wynton, Branford),
John Scofield and Jim Hall,
Kenny Werner, Billy Cobham,

Don Thompson, Terry Clark,
Marshall Royal and Snooky Young,
Lawrence Brown and Herman Riley,

Rufus Reid and Billy Hart
with Tommy Flanagan,
Ray Brown, James Williams plus Tal Farlow,

Bob Maize and Pat Martino,
Jake Hanna, Bobby McFerrin,
Astrud Gilberto, Little Queenie

and the Percolators,
Ray Walker, Gary France
(who played with her in Perth),

Al Heath, Jay Ashby plus Herb Ellis,
all names we've heard, or think we've heard,
and some won't recognise,

recorded often or slipped by
  without much smell of vinyl.
all of them onstage with Em,

standing back to hear her solo
or, close behind her, keeping up
the thrust that leads to lift-off.

At other times, guitarist duos,
trading back and forth,
moments of pure colloquy

resolving into smiles.

17.

*But at 29, I think now I'm ready to be more focussed and to learn
the business a little better.*

All those gigs and all those airports,
the smell of kerosene,
the checking of guitars and amps,

the set-up or a run-through
top-and-tail before they're on,
the drummer and the bassist,

temperaments unknown,
though idols to a hundred fans,
musicians who've declined to tour,

who've chosen not to risk the 'Apple'.
They have their reasons though
as Emily can see.

Wes Montgomery himself
was one of those who stayed back home
for years in Indianapolis

with eight kids to support,
a factory job to make ends meet.
Em's been a 'freelance all these years'

along with all the others like her —
too hard to keep a quartet working
and flying it about.

Often, but not always,
there's a boyfriend in New York,
who may be missing her.

The trips reach out across the States
and Europe in the summer.
In 1989 she takes

a freelance tour 'Down Under'.
The guys have got the chops, she's told;
they know her records too.

To be American down there
always brings a little cachet.
A woman 'on the road'

is something else again.
Em's learned now how to feel
her audiences out,

to re-arrange a set list
as cirumstance requires
though not *too* far away from what's

already been agreed:
standards in the standard key,
a tag or vamp tacked on,

arranged that afternoon.
When Em's on-stage it's all OK
or nearly always. Afterwards,

there'll be these half-assed guys around,
fancying their chances.
And after that the flights, the nights,

the days between that slowly build
a lonely sort of pressure.
At some point, heroin becomes

an easy velvet room for later,
the ultimate relaxant.
She almost certainly knows guys

who've used it half their lives.
It's not a 'habit' yet, she's sure.
Just 'every now and then'.

The gear's not hard to find.
Rumours tend to seek her out.
Dealers turn up at her gigs

not always for the music.

18.

I may look like a nice Jewish girl from New Jersey ...

Mythologised while still alive.
The journalists can't help themselves,
besetting her for self-description,

the 'how are you so good so soon?',
the 'how do you survive?'
(when all the gods are male)

the 'Jewish girl' who 'went to Berklee',
who used to be 'bohemian',
who called herself a 'hippie' —

before she knuckled down
all through that hot and fabled summer
beside the Jersey shore.

In 1982,
for People Magazine,
she offers up the famous quote,

the one about how 'deep down' she's
'a black man', 'heavy-set', 'at 50'
'a thumb like Wes Montomery's'.

But Wes had died at 45,
fourteen years before,
the thumb employed for late-night practice

so as not to stress the neighbours.
He held that factory day job too
to see eight kids through school.

Later, Wes's friends recalled
that happy house of daughters.
Music wasn't all he lived for.

He'd toured with Hampton years before
but 'Naptown' was his home.
Like Emily, his time in lights

lasted just ten years.
Emily claims in interviews
she 'knows' the masters she's not met

entirely through their records.
Her studies lead her to the essence
but not, perhaps, the context.

The 1980s are for her
a milieu of their own.
Her tributes though are genuine.

She knows precisely what she offers.

19.

I'm sort of proud of my teaching abilities ...

Even in New Orleans, aged
nineteen, Emily has students —
25, in fact.

She remembers how she learned
and therefore how to teach.
For her, it's not an irritation or

a second string for money.
She knows exactly where to start
and what each student needs.

'If their rhythm is bad we work on rhythm.
If their rhythm is good we'll start on theory'.
And always there's the metronome.

Can't say enough on that.
She knows she used to 'rush' a lot,
back when she was seventeen.

Two bars, four bars. She well knows
'too much will not sink in'.
'I work on blues first,' she's telling *Downbeat*

magazine in '85.
She makes those teaching videos
still viewable on YouTube.

Bebop & Swing Guitar, Advanced
Jazz & Latin Improvisation.
Em stares directly from the screen

and sets you straight on bossa.
Don't mess with one and three, she says.
No syncopation there.

She talks about the minor scale,
its variant in jazz,
the one with sharpened sixths

when running up and down
and how when started from the fifth
it yields the sharp eleventh.

'Lydian spice', she likes to say.
At Pittsburg she does lots of teaching
and not a little learning too.

'She lived in Pittsburg's Squirrel Hall,'
her student, Edward Barr, recalls,
briskly turning up at seven

every fortnight in the morning,
already in his business suit
and Em still in her 'nightshirt'

drinking herbal tea.
Although they talked for half an hour
she 'hammered away at the fundamentals',

always adding something extra,
a 'favourite lick' maybe.
'She taught me to be confident,

to play "wrong but strong" if I had to.'
'Don't be timid. Practise loud,'
Another student, Joel Turoff,

drives across from Cleveland
'every few months' to take a class,
recording it for later

with Em's encouragement.
They too survive on YouTube,
just the voices and guitars

like neighbours through a wall.
'What are you going to do, stop playing,'
she chivvies Edward Barr,

'every time you make a mistake
or a drunk falls off a stool?'
Then adds, with prescience:

'The music will go on without you,
whether you're brilliant or dumb.'
In NYC another would-be,

Michael Ducey, calls to mind
a lesson he once had with Em,
on crutches with her leg in plaster,

and how that night he piggybacked her
through the streets of Greenwich Village,
to get her to the Blue Note where

they caught the Joe Pass / Jim Hall duo.
Teaching, learning, playing
were all a part of it, the on-

stage bit just slightly more important.

20.

And I'll probably be doing another one in a little while.

Carl Jefferson of Concord Records
signs her up in '81.
Firefly is the first one out,

the title track a tribute to
her Master of the Octaves.
An interview in '86

concedes it's 'straight ahead'.
'Demure' might be more apposite,
considering what's yet to come.

There is a song by Horace Silver,
a not well-known Jobim,
and 'In a Sentimental Mood'

tossed in to wrap it up.
The highpoint though's 'The Firefly',
fast and energised, another

homage played for Wes.
Even her illustrious
companions, rich with longer wisdom,

contribute to the mood
of cautious expertise.
Skip ahead to '88,

the album *East Meets Wes*.
Hank Jones again (piano),
Buster Williams (bass)

and Martin 'Smitty' Smith (on drums)
contrive to bring it right up close.
The room is all bravura.

The microphones are gathered tight;
there's impetus, variety —
and still the wave to Wes.

Clifford Brown's 'Dahoud'
sparks the whole thing off.
Emily shares Clifford's fleetness —

or quite a bit thereof.
Aficionados don't forget
that pair of early deaths:

Clifford on the turnpike,
aged just twenty-six.
Emily, in Sydney, touring,

not yet 33.
'Hot House' by Tadd Dameron
makes another nod to bebop.

But this is not nostalgia only.
The '70s are there as well,
a touch of Larry Coryell

with 'Snowfall' on the second track.

Later on, the twenties classic
'Softly as a Morning Sunrise' —

cleverly reworked.
She's stretching out and in control,
thoughtful but spontaneous.

'East to Wes', the final track,
is offered as a last salute,
those octaves in her final eight.

Six discs straight in seven years
still seems a healthy run
and some of them remain on sale

unshadowed by her death.
More notable again
is what Gene Lees recalls.

November 14, '87,
an unnamed club in Pittsburg where
he goes back 'two more nights' to catch

'the sheer strength of her playing',
so different from the albums which
he calls 'conservative'.

Live, he's hearing Emily
'edging close to ... avant-garde',
a 'daring' player who

'swung ferociously'.
In '86 she's telling

Martin Richards that

her albums were all 'six hour sessions'
which discontents her 'picky self'.
'Tunes' are no big deal, she says.

'Compositions' need more time
to find precisely what you want.
Those records are the record now,

continuing and fixed.

21.

You know what my dream is? My dream is to write for the
movies, like John Williams.

And in her final album,
This Is Me, on Justice Records,
she takes a step towards it:

synthesisers, Latin touch,
sparse and simple intervals,
the synthesisers hoping

to sound like tiers of strings,
cellos, violins and violas,
delivering instead

the sound an elevator offers
rising to a higher floor.
She likes the scale of movie music,

the wide-screen stretch of sound.
The money too, she surely thinks,
remembering the jazz clubs

with maybe fifty devotees
nursing single drinks.
But, as she says in '82,

'You can't be in jazz for the money.'
Though *This Is Me* proves posthumous
it's clear she heard the takes.

The disc's executive producer
insists that Emily
truly 'loved this record'

and thought it 'only the beginning'
of something new 'in her career'.
This Is Me, the album's billed ...

and gets it wrong entirely.
This Is Me (Pursuing Money)
might be more accurate

although the confidence is there.
She knows exactly what she's at.
We're lifted upwards, off to heaven

or Hollywood at best.

22.

In most major cities there are some very competent people and
you learn from them as you go ...

'89, the northern spring
and Em's away 'Down Under',
Australia and New Zealand,

touring as a single.
She has a manager by now,
the son of Tony Bennett,

a kid she went to high school with,
who manages his dad as well.
It must be he who handles

faxes and the phone,
who gets the news on which musicians
occupy her league,

the ones who've got the chops and knowledge
despite their being so far off,
residing at the end

of all those hours of flight.
He'll book the hotels too
or line up people she can stay with.

Ed Gaston would be one,
the bassist from North Carolina,
who's been down there for decades now.

There'll be the pressure of the planes,
the sound-checks and the run-throughs with
musicians not yet met,

a few of whom will know her records
and others maybe not.
'It's not the worst experience,'

Emily will say of tours
around the States and Europe.
'Down Under' is a longer hop.

The venues there are well stretched out:
Adelaide and Sydney,
Brisbane and the Gold Coast —

with Perth as well, five further hours.
Sometimes there's a workshop too;
she's always been a teacher.

The accent may be different but
the language is the same
i.e. chords and standards with

at times a switch of key.
There's been a set-list sent by fax.
And one or two originals,

assuming time permits.
The gigs require them all to wing it.
The night itself is improvised,

their solos just a part of that
prolonged improvisation
musicians know as life.

This time though the Midday Show
gives the tour a nudge.
Ray Martin is the host.

Cameras circle round their prey
as Ray spells out a row of gigs;
then calls the tune as 'Tenor Madness'.

He may not have the records but
he shows enough respect.
Emily is in a dress

with squares of different colours,
long sleeves to the wrist.
She flicks a nervous smile and then

it's on — piano, bass and drums —
the head played twice and then guitar,
four times through in all,

and two more for the pianist;
then back to Emily who plays
two choruses in octaves

before they check the head again.
She's done this sort of thing so often —
it nearly always works out fine.

There may have been another take
but we're thinking that's unlikely.
The job is done; she's on her way.

The rest is flights and taxis.

23.

*It's great to be here in Perth and I really like it so much I'm
telling people I want to move here* (laughs).

Here she is in Perth at last,
as far away from New York as
it's possible to get

unless you count the moon.
It's May 8, 1989.
We're at Hyde Park Hotel.

She joins three locals on the stage:
Ray Walker on guitar;
Brian Bursey on the bass and Gary

France on drums — 'from Syracuse,
New York,' as Emily will wisecrack
later. There is a bootleg of it,

never quite released.
The tape is fine except the cymbals
aren't recorded right.

Ray Walker is on rhythm but
he gets his solo share.
It can be hard to tell between them

but Emily's the one who mainly
takes the greater risks.
As in 'Tenor Madness',

the tune she left on YouTube.
The Perth take proves a little wilder,
no cameras dollying about,

just a room that has the knowledge.
This trio on the western edge
of what jazz means around the world

is more than satisfied to have
a visit from the core,
this lady with technique to burn,

who knows her bossa nova,
who makes it seem as if the ghost
of Wes is sitting in.

The set-list's unremarkable
but none the worse for that:
songs from Hollywood and Broadway

('Yesterdays' and 'Softly as ...',
'What's New?' and 'Secret Love');
two bossas by Jobim

('Triste', 'How Insensitive')
two tunes from Miles and Sonny Rollins
('All Blues', 'Tenor Madness').

Plus some Monk and Clifford Brown.
'Days of Wine and Roses' too,
sadder now in retrospect,

considering the film.
The tape is raw, unedited.
We hear the space between the songs,

her off-mike chatter with the guys,
calling tunes and keys and tempos.
Emily's announcements,

properly preserved,
are wry and humorous at times
and not at all ungrateful that

this room so distant from Manhattan
has understood so much.
She hears it in the clapping surely,

a whistle here and there,
set off by pure intensities
unforeseen or willed.

They clap her back to do an encore
(Bill Evans' 'Funkallero');
someone else who died too soon.

The voice that bids the crowd goodnight
is young and sure, as if it had
another fifty years to run.

Gary France that night could see
no sign, although he knew the rumours.
'Friendly', 'Nice', 'Always supportive'

'No dirty looks,' he says.

24.

I live on cheese omelets. I take in a lot of chloresterol — it's good
for sliding up and down the guitar neck. And the caffeine's good for
speed and ability, and the bagels and cream cheese are good for the
creative end of it.

Back home in June that year,
she's talking on the phone
to Philadelphia,

Nels Nelson, journalist and fan.
He starts with where she's living,
Sheepshead Bay in Brooklyn —

cheerful domesticity,
close beside the sea.
He flirts with her a little, asking

why her photos look so different
every time he checks.
She jokes about her weight.

Within the year we know she'll die
in Sydney from a 'heart attack',
according to the New York Times.

May 3, 1990,
some time in the early morning.
That's the version given out,

the doctor's slip of paper.
That second tour 'Down Under'
left little paperwork.

Had she played the other dates
or were they still to come?
We know she did the gig in Sydney;

we know, or think we know,
Ed Gaston was the bassist.
We know that she'd been asked to stay

by Gaston and his wife, Dianne,
out of friendship — or to save
on touring costs perhaps.

Gene Lees, who'd seen injection scars
'like tiny railroad tracks',
locates it in a 'hotel room'.

That makes it all more mythical
and later proves untrue.
Ed Gaston, or Dianne, his wife,

finds her in the bathroom,
not their only one perhaps,
already dead that autumn morning.

The gossip talks of delaudid
as well as heroin,
the former much more powerful,

especially uncut,
more suppressive of the systems,
more like a heart attack maybe.

Reports don't mention a syringe.
Emily's 'official' site
allthingsemily.com

concedes that drugs 'contributed'.
It's notable just how
in all the interviews she gave

the word is not heard once.
Heart attacks at 32
are rare but not unknown.

While travelling with Coryell
she'd noticed how he'd always
jog and watch his diet.

She'd joked about cholesterol.
Her dresses had long sleeves at times
but in the photos for that final

problematic album
she wears a summer tanktop.
Either way, each truth is brutal.

One, she's shooting up alone
in someone else's bathroom,
friends she's spent the evening with,

the bassist in her pick-up group.
In that scenario
she feels the rush then starts to nod,

foreshadowing a sleep,
some temporary obliteration
she'll climb from in an hour or two

or with the dawn at Connells Point.
Or two, the heart attack would be
a lot less quick. Why wasn't there

the time to stagger out for help?
We try to re-construct her thoughts:
Fuck's sake, I'm only 32

What's this clawing at my ribs?
I've still got so much more to do.
'I'd like to make a contribution,'

she'd said in '85
and in those dizzying few seconds
(minutes?) knows she has and hasn't

done what ten years more,
or even thirty-five,
would surely have permitted.

'You get to be afraid of balance,
of mediocrity,'
she'd told Gene Lees in '87.

Does she cry out mutely for
her boyfriend back on Sheepshead Bay?
The cause of death should be, we say,

irrelevant. Let's hold the music
only, remembered in the minds
of all who heard her play,

who in their turn will mostly face,
or have by now already faced,
more gracious and more timely deaths

and not so far from home.

Acknowledgements

This elegy, in the apparent absence of a full-length prose biography, is based almost entirely on materials available on the internet, many of them from, or linked to, the 'official' Emily Remler website, *allthingsemily.com* They include, among others, the relevant essay in Gene Lees' book, *Waiting for Dizzy* (1991). I have endeavoured to adhere to the facts as they are known but inevitably there must be speculation about motives, the nature of relationships and, ultimately, some of the 'facts' themselves.

I'd like to thank guitarist, Victor Rufus, who checked parts of the manuscript for technical accuracy. Keith Penhallow made some useful suggestions and corrections. Gary France kindly shared his memories of playing with Emily Remler in Perth, W.A.

I should also thank the Austalian Defence Force Academy where I have been an honorary visiting fellow for many years.

Lastly, I thank my former partner, Alison Hastie, for her proofreading and so much else.

Emily Remler Discography

As Leader
Firefly (Concord Jazz, 1981)
Take Two (Concord Jazz, 1982)
Transitions (Concord Jazz, 1984)
Catwalk (Concord Jazz 1985)
Together :With Larry Coryell (Concord Jazz, 1985)
East to Wes (Concord Jazz, 1988)
This is Me (Justice Records, 1990)
Emily Remler: Retrospective Volume One: Standards (Concord Jazz, 1991)
Emily Remler: Retrospective Volume Two: Compositions (Concord Jazz, 1991)

With Others
All in the Family: The Clayton Brothers (Concord Jazz, 1981)
Soular Energy: Ray Brown (Concord Jazz, 1984)
No More Blues : Susannah McCorkle (Concord Jazz, 1988)